30119 025 387 384

Mum's New Hat

Roderick Hunt • Alex Brychta

D1333389

OXFORD
UNIVERSITY PRESS

Mum had a new hat.

The wind blew.

It blew Mum's hat off.

"Get my hat," said Mum.

Dad ran.

The wind blew.

Oh no!

"Get that hat," said Dad.

Kipper ran.

The wind blew.

Oh no!

"Get that hat," said Kipper.

Biff ran.

The wind blew.

Oh no!

"Look at my new hat!"
said Mum.

Think about the story

How did Mum lose her new hat?

Why do you think Biff has a camera?

What funny things happened to Mum's hat?

What has happened to you on windy days?

A maze

Help Mum get her hat.

Useful common words repeated in this story and other books at Level 1.

get   my   said   the

Names in this story: Mum   Dad   Biff   Kipper